Curaçao

by George S. Lewbel, Ph.D.,
and the editors of Pisces Books

Photography by Larry R. Martin
and George S. Lewbel, Ph.D.

Pisces Books • New York

Acknowledgments

The author very much appreciates the assistance of Mssrs. Larry R. Martin and Gregory S. Boland of LGL Ecological Research Associates; Mssrs. Elio Romijn and Eitel Hernandez and the Curacao Tourist Bureau; Mr. Ludwig K. Loy and ALM Antillean Airlines; Drs. Tom van't Hof and Jeff Sybesma, and the Netherlands Antilles National Parks Foundation (STINAPA); Mssrs. Oswaldo Serberie and Erold Martina, and Dive Curacao & Watersports; Mr. van der Horst and the Princess Beach Hotel; Mssrs. Frank Engelhardt, Marlon Panka, Eric Sperwer, Franklin Ietswaart, and Master-dive Scubashop; Mr. Harry C. Aarsse and Coral Cliff Resort & Beach Club; Mr. Ben van Dalen of Piscadera Watersports; and Mr. Charles Gustavson and Ms. Kris Gustavson.

Publishers Note: At the time of publication of this book, all the information was determined to be as accurate as possible. However, when you use this guide, new construction may have changed land reference points, weather may have altered reef configurations, and some businesses may no longer be functioning. Your assistance in keeping future editions up-to-date will be greatly appreciated.

Also, please pay particular attention to the diver rating system in this book. Know your limits!

Library of Congress Cataloging-in-Publication Data
Lewbel, George S.
  Diving and snorkeling guide to Curaçao.
  Includes index.
  1. Skin diving—Curaçao—Guide-books. 2. Curaçao—Description and travel—Guide books. I. Martin, Larry R. II. Pisces Books (Firm) III. Title.
GV840.S78L492 1988   797.2'3'0972986   88-6022
ISBN 0-86636-085-9

Cover photo by L.R. Martin.

Printed in Hong Kong

10 9 8 7 6 5 4 3 2 1

Table of Contents

How to Use This Guide

This guide will acquaint you with a variety of dive sites on Curaçao and provide information that you can use to decide whether or not a particular site is appropriate for your abilities and intended dive plan. If you arrive ready to jump in the water, you'll find dive-by-dive descriptions in Chapter 2, Diving on Curaçao. Read the entire chapter before selecting a site, since some material that is common to several sites is not repeated for each one. Chapter 3, Safety, should be read first, because it covers both routine and emergency procedures.

Sooner or later, you'll have to put in some surface time to get rid of that excess nitrogen you've built up underwater or to let your skin dry out. On early trips to the Netherlands Antilles, I tried to keep that surface interval short because the diving was so good, but looking back on those trips I'd have to admit that I shortchanged myself. The Netherlands Antilles are extremely interesting islands with spectacular scenery both above and below the water line. Where else in the Caribbean can you find wild parrots nesting in cactus, limestone caves with growing stalactites and crystalline pools, lunar landscapes, and coral reefs, as well as a friendly populace that speaks four languages? Chapter 1, Overview of Curaçao, offers a description of the island's history, geography, scenery, and some general information on accommodations, services other than diving, and shopping. Appendix I is a selected list of hotels, dive shops, and dive operators, and will be helpful to you if you need to make your own hotel and diving arrangements on arrival.

Most of the drop-offs on Curaçao have fairly gentle slopes. Photo: L. R. Martin.

The Rating System for Divers and Dives

A conventional rating system (novice, intermediate, advanced) is really not practical on a site-by-site basis for most locations on Curaçao. Curaçao has a fringing reef that starts on a shelf or submarine terrace near shore, curls over a lip at depths ranging from 20 to 40 feet (6–12 meters) and then continues down a sloping drop-off. Nearly every site therefore includes good shallow-water diving on the terrace and on deeper areas over the lip; a description of typical dive depth would be meaningless for most sites.

We do have some recommendations as to which parts of the typical reef profile are suitable for divers of various skill levels, though. Inexperienced divers should never place themselves in any situation where loss of bouyancy control could result in rapid depth increases. This translates as advice to keep away from walls (that is, near-vertical or vertical drop-offs). Diving on or near walls is considered safe only for advanced divers, or for intermediate divers under proper supervision. Gradual drop-offs present less hazard, and diving on or below the lip of these drop-offs (slopes less steep than 45°) is considered safe for well-supervised novices. The word supervised should be understood to mean that a diver is under the direct supervision of a qualified instructor or divemaster.

These recommendations should be taken in a conservative sense keeping in mind the old adage about there being old divers and bold divers but few old bold divers. It is assumed that any diver using this guide is in decent physical condition. A novice diver is defined as a diver who has recently completed a basic certification sport diving course, or a certified sport diver who has not been diving recently or who has no experience in similar waters. An intermediate diver is defined as a certified sport diver who has been diving actively for at least a year following a basic course, and who has been diving recently in similar waters. An advanced diver is defined as someone who has completed an advanced certification sport diving course, and who has been diving recently in similar waters.

You will have to decide yourself, of course, if you are capable of making any particular dive depending on your level of training, recency of experience, physical condition, and on the water conditions at the site. Remember that water conditions can change at any time, even during a dive. Penetration of wrecks, diving in caverns or caves, or diving below a depth of 100 feet (30 meters) is considered to be suitable only for advanced divers with specialized training in these skills. Diving below a depth of 130 feet (40 meters) is considered to be outside the realm of sport diving.

Christmas tree worms (Spirobranchus giganteus) *grow on fire coral* (Millepora complanata) *at Wetsuit City. Photo: G. S. Lewbel.*

Fire coral (Millepora complanata) *forms delicate plates in shallow water at Wet Suit City. Photo: G. S. Lewbel.*

1

Overview of Curaçao

History. Curaçao Island (pronounced cur-ah-sow) is the largest of the five Netherlands Antilles islands. The Netherlands Antilles include Bonaire and Curaçao—which lies within sight of Venezuela, and three smaller islands, St. Maarten, Saba, and St. Eustatius, 600 miles (960 kilometers) to the north. Curaçao is 38 miles (60 kilometers) long and 7 miles (11 kilometers) wide, and its capital, Willemstad, is the seat of government for the five islands and the largest town in the islands.

Curaçao has been politically, economically, and militarily valuable for over four hundred years despite its virtual lack of most natural resources. It has been important primarily because it has a large protected harbor where large warships can be anchored and guarded. This anchorage (St. Anna Baai and Schottegat) has been in demand since the early sixteenth century. When other countries squabbled for supremacy on the high seas, control of Curaçao's harbor was one of the keys to power in the Caribbean. Curaçao's history is therefore more complex than you might expect for such a seemingly remote island. Indeed, Curaçao's present-day diversity is the happy end-product of that complicated history.

Before their discovery by Europeans, the islands were inhabited by the Caiquetios, a tribe of Arawak Indians. Their traces remain in the form of pictographs painted with red dye in various caves. The islands were discovered in 1499 by a Spanish expedition whose navigator was Amerigo Vespucci, for whom America was named. The islands were claimed by the Spanish from their discovery in 1499 until 1634, although the Spanish initially considered the islands useless because they lacked precious metals. Unfortunately, the Spanish did not feel the same about the Caiquetios and deported all but a handful of the 2,000 inhabitants to work in the copper mines in Santo Domingo. The Spanish then converted Curaçao into a ranching island by bringing in cattle and sheep. Curaçao was also used as a port by slavers who captured mainland Indians.

Spanish colonial rule of Curaçao ended in 1634 when the Dutch, involved in a war with Spain, took the island. Over the next two centuries, the Dutch built four forts—Fort Amsterdam, Waterfort, Riffort, and Fort Nassau—to protect St. Anna Baai. When the war ended in 1648, the islands remained Dutch colonies.

Being isolated in the south central Caribbean, Curaçao offers a diversity of marine life that matches the best Caribbean locations.

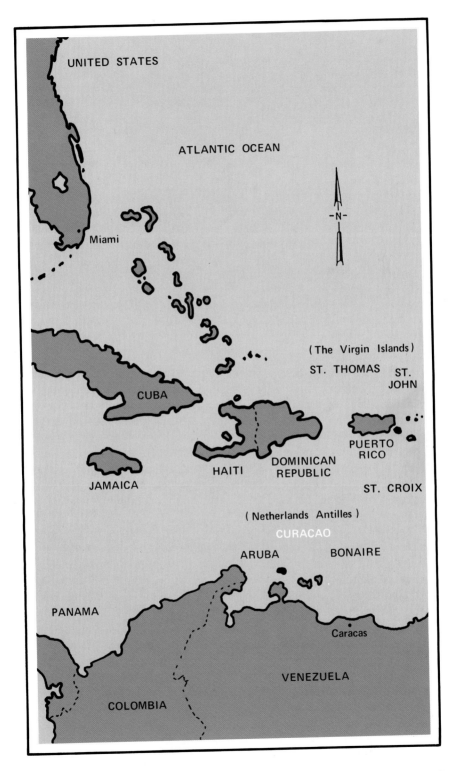

UNITED STATES

ATLANTIC OCEAN

-N-

Miami

(The Virgin Islands)

ST. THOMAS   ST.
JOHN

CUBA

PUERTO
RICO

HAITI   DOMINICAN
             REPUBLIC

JAMAICA

ST. CROIX

(Netherlands Antilles)

CURACAO

ARUBA   BONAIRE

PANAMA

Caracas

VENEZUELA

COLOMBIA

Knipbaai on a rough day. Photo: G. S. Lewbel.

The Dutch became heavily involved in the black slave trade during the seventeenth century. Curaçao was used as a major stopover and transhipment location by slavers from Africa, whose human cargo was allowed to rest and regain some strength after the brutal Atlantic crossing. Elegant plantation houses (landhuizen) were constructed as status symbols and staffed with slaves, although it was all but impossible to raise most crops on the arid land. Some of these landhuizen have been preserved as historical monuments and can be visited today by tourists. The slave trade continued to flourish on the island until the mid-eighteenth century and was not officially abolished until 1864.

Despite their acceptance of slavery, the Dutch were tolerant of differing religious and political views. The Netherlands Antilles sheltered refugees from all over the world. Many Jews, fleeing religious persecution during the eighteenth century, emigrated to Curaçao from the Netherlands and from Brazil. The Brazilian Jews spoke Portuguese, as did the coastal slave traders. Traces of this heritage can be found in one of the island languages, Papiamento (also spelled Papiamentu), a Portuguese-based mixture that includes some Spanish, Dutch, English, and African words. There is still a large Jewish population on Curaçao, and Mikvé Israël Synagogue is the oldest synagogue in the western hemisphere. The Dutch Catholic church sent missionaries to convert African slaves to Christianity, and evidence of their work is still present; most of Curaçao's residents are Catholic.

The modern period for Curaçao began with the arrival of the oil industry. Due (once again) to the need for a safe harbor, Royal Dutch Shell built a refinery in 1915 in Schottegat to process and store oil from Venezuela. Modernization and industrialization soon followed. Shell Curaçao was the single largest employer on the island for many years. When World War II broke out, the Shell refinery became a crucial link in the supply of petroleum to the Allies, and Curaçao drew closer economically to the United States.

Shell sold the refinery in 1985 to the Netherlands Antilles Government who in turn leased it to an affiliate of Petroleos de Venezuela S.A., the official oil exploration and production agency of the Venezuelan government. Although its economic importance to islanders has been reduced due to automation and the worldwide decline in petroleum prices, the refinery remains the single largest employer on Curaçao.

The island is rapidly expanding its capabilities for tourism, and many locals feel that divers and beach-goers may be its most reliable source of foreign exchange and income in the future.

The Netherlands Antilles were granted formal independence from the Kingdom of the Netherlands in 1954, but are still closely associated with the Dutch government and economy. A democratically-elected parliament (de Staten) handles issues affecting all of the islands, while each of the islands has its own separate government to deal with local affairs. At the time of independence, the Netherlands Antilles included Aruba, Bonaire, Curaçao, St. Maarten, Saba, and St. Eustatius. Aruba severed its political ties with the Netherlands Antilles in January, 1986, but the other five islands remain together in the alliance.

The modern and the antique come together in the harbor at Willemstad. The red roofs of traditional Dutch buildings contrast with waterfront highrises. Photo: L. R. Martin.

Curaçao Island Today

If you're the same way I am about diving, you probably hope to spend the maximum amount of time underwater with the minimum surface interval before getting back in again. Fortunately, if you're doing any shore diving you'll have to drive through the Curaçao countryside to get to the good spots. It's worth the time—even if you miss a morning's dive—to roam around the island by car. Curaçao is completely different from the usual lush Caribbean island many visitors expect. It has large sections of extremely rugged desert terrain, small rural villages, and a surprisingly sophisticated modern city, Willemstad, with a population of over 165,000.

Curaçao is a dry, hilly island. It has volcanic baserock which is capped in most places by limestone, the remains of ancient coral reefs. This limestone is continually being slowly dissolved and eroded. The process of dissolution results in many underground caves and caverns. Above ground and along the shore, erosion leaves limestone with very sharp edges. At the beach, eroded limestone is referred to as "ironshore", and you'll need wet suit boots and gloves to get over it safely where there isn't any sand.

Although there are palm trees here and there, and orchids grow on the sides of some of the higher hills, most of the natural vegetation is cactus and thorn bushes. You've probably seen various extracts of aloe vera for sale as a soothing skin lotion or remedy for sunburn; the aloe plant from which the sap is extracted grows all over Curaçao and was once raised there on large plantations. The plants look like yuccas with thick, long, pointed green leaves.

Many dive locations on Curaçao can be reached by a short swim from the beach. Photo: L. R. Martin.

Paperwork. A word to the wise about documentation and international travel is included here. To get into the Netherlands Antilles from the United States, you'll need some proof of citizenship such as a birth certificate, passport, or voter's registration card, and a return ticket. You'll then be issued a temporary visa card, which you'll have to surrender to get out of the country. If you're bringing minors along, and both parents aren't accompanying the minor(s), bring a notarized letter from the absent parent giving you permission to take the child to the Netherlands Antilles for a vacation. When you leave the Netherlands Antilles, there is a tax (about $8 US in 1988) at the airport, so save some money for your departure.

Climate. The climate in the Netherlands Antilles is extremely predictable: windy and warm, or very windy and warm. The islands lie beneath the trade winds, which blow from the east 24 hours a day, year-round. The weather is best for diving in the summer and fall. During the first half of the year, especially from January through April, wind velocities are highest and water roughest in unprotected locations. This is a consideration for divers bound for Curaçao.

Humidity is low compared to most tropical places —hence the desert vegetation. Average daytime temperatures are in the mid-eighties (about 30°C), but the constant breeze will keep you cool in most locations. Occasional rainshowers are most common in the afternoons, but annual rainfall in the islands is only about 22 inches (55 cm). It's rarely cold enough in the evening to require anything but a light wrap or long-sleeved shirt. The climate is one of the finest in the Caribbean. Daytime as well as nighttime dress on Curaçao is casual.

Antipatharian wire corals may be seen in deeper water along the drop-off. Photo: G. S. Lewbel.

Foreign Exchange. The unit of currency in the Netherlands Antilles is the guilder, abbreviated Naf., which is further divided into 100 cents. As of 1988, $1 US was worth about 1.7 to 1.8 guilders, depending on where you exchanged your money. American dollars are accepted nearly everywhere, though the exchange rate you're offered at hotels, restaurants, or stores may be a few cents less than at the bank.

Credit cards such as American Express, Mastercard, and Visa are accepted by most businesses, but there can be a few surprises for Americans using their credit cards in the Netherlands Antilles. You are probably aware that the company that issued your credit card also charges merchants about 3%–4% of the total bill when you use it. It's not uncommon for businesses on Curaçao to add that percentage to your charges to cover their expenses. If you want to use your credit card to pay your hotel bill, notify the hotel several days before you check out, or you may find that it won't be accepted as you're running for the airport.

Tipping. Tipping in the Netherlands Antilles is similar to tipping in the U. S. The range for excellent service is 10–15 percent with trades relying on tips being those that cater to travelers, such as taxi drivers. Most restaurants add a service charge to your bill as a sort of mandatory tip, so be sure to take a look at the charges before you leave any extra cash.

Typical back-country vegetation on Curacao. Photo: G.S. Lewbel.

A banded coral shrimp (Stenopus hispidus) *waits for customers at a cleaning station. Photo: G. S. Lewbel.*

A Caution Regarding Electric and Electronic Devices. Although the electric outlets in hotels on Curaçao are supposed to put out between 110 and 130 volts AC, the amount actually supplied varies from 100 volts during periods of heavy use to 140 volts or more when things are quiet. In addition, electricity is supplied at 50 cycles per second Hz, not 60 (as in the States). These differences may not seem very important, but they are.

Electronic devices such as radios may be insensitive to the difference in voltage when the supply is less than 120 volts. Appliances that have motors in them, such as razors and hair dryers, often run more slowly than normal when supplied at 50 Hz. Although they're spinning slower, they overheat because they're being fed at higher voltages.

Be extremely careful about plugging your strobe or flashlight charger into ordinary outlets. Chargers designed for 60 Hz will have a drastically reduced output at 50 Hz, and may take two to four times as long as normal to charge your strobe. Be sure to check your charger frequently to make sure it's not too hot, and if the lights in your room suddenly get brighter, unplug your charger immediately or it may turn into a melted block of plastic. Most of the dive operators have a voltage-limited set of outlets specifically for use with chargers, and you are strongly urged to take advantage of them.

Shopping and Dining. Most hotel rooms, restaurants, dive shops, car rental agencies, the Curaçao Tourist Board (an excellent source of information on the island), camera stores, and so forth are in Willemstad. The best way to find most of these services is to pick up a copy of Curaçao Holiday, a newspaper-like publication distributed all over the island for free to tourists.

Willemstad is a bustling city of commerce and industry, dominated by the Shell refinery and associated petroleum storage tanks and related facilities. Built around the old harbor of St. Anna Baai, the city is divided roughly in half by the entrance to the Bay with the two halves linked by bridges. The eastern half, called the Punda, is where most of the historic buildings are located.

English is spoken by nearly everyone. You'll have no difficulty coping with menus, which are usually printed in at least two or three languages in larger restaurants. You will find a good selection of restaurants with seafood an island specialty. Rijsttafel, an Indonesian specialty consisting of a dozen or more tasty small dishes served on a bed of rice, is served proudly by many restaurants. Restaurants range from simple to haute cuisine. If you're addicted to American fast food, you'll find McDonald's, Pizza Hut, Kentucky Fried Chicken, and other such shops in Willemstad. Jamoca almond fudge junkies can take heart: there are Baskin-Robbins ice cream stores in Willemstad, too!

The swinging pontoon bridge across the entrance to St. Anna Baai. Photo: G. S. Boland.

Hotels. There are four hotels on the island that are thoroughly committed to diving programs and have dive shops on the premises. All of them are on the water and tend to be luxurious by Caribbean standards. They have air-conditioning, restaurants, and other conveniences in addition to the obvious advantages of having a dive shop at hand.

The Princess Beach Hotel & Casino houses Dive Curaçao and Watersports. The Princess Beach is on the eastern edge of Willemstad, next door to the Seaquarium where Underwater Curaçao and Masterdive's retail shop are head-quartered. The Curaçao Caribbean (formerly the Curaçao Concorde) hosts Piscadera Watersports and is located on Piscadera Bay, just west of Willemstad. The Coral Cliff Resort & Beach Club is where Coral Cliff Diving is located. The Coral Cliff has the most spectacular setting, although it is the farthest from town. Most rooms have kitchens.

There are also numerous small hotels in town and nearby, most of which are less expensive—and, of course, less fancy—than the four mentioned above. Nearly all of them are air-conditioned and equipped with modern facilities. You'll have ready access to restaurants and shops, though you may not be right on the water. If you don't stay at a hotel with a dive operator, you may not need a rental car. Most of the dive operators can arrange hotel pickups for boat dives.

The Avila Beach is one of the nicest, most comfortable hotels in town and is on the beach. The Las Palmas has their own dive operation, the Las Palmas Reef Divers. The Las Palmas is more rustic, with cottages and a fine view, and is just a stone's throw from the Curaçao Caribbean. Others include the Hotel Holland, the Park Hotel, and the Trupial Inn. The Park Hotel is usually the least expensive of these, lacking both pool and beach. The Avila Beach, Las Palmas, and Trupial Inn offer kitchens. Since restaurant meals on Curaçao are typically costly, the ability to prepare your own meals may be an important consideration if you're on a tight budget.

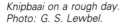
*Knipbaai on a rough day.
Photo: G. S. Lewbel.*

Transportation. On many Caribbean islands a car is not essential because of the nature of dive operators and sites, the difficulty of driving in a foreign country, and the cost. On Curaçao, however, you'll miss some of the best beach diving—and the most interesting scenery—in the world if you don't arrange for transportation to the back country. Furthermore, if you arrive during the windy season and can't go boat diving, your only practical means of getting into the water will be to drive out to the protected coves of the northwest side of the island.

For non-diving transportation, there are shuttles from the outlying hotels into Willemstad, though the schedules may not suit you since they are designed mainly for casino-goers rather than divers. There are also many taxis within Willemstad, and they have reasonable prices.

Your valid driver's license from the U.S. will be sufficient for driving a rental car, and any hotel can make the arrangements if you don't have one reserved ahead of your arrival. The major car rental companies (for example, National, Avis, or Budget) do business on Curaçao, so you can reserve one before leaving home. Keep in mind that international road signs are used, so if you're not familiar with them, ask the car rental agent to explain them to you before setting out. Don't forget that speed limits are in kilometers per hour. Within towns the speed limit is 40 kph; outside of towns, it's 60 kph unless otherwise posted. Drive on the right-hand side of the road, as in the States, and be careful of one-way roads. There are lots of them.

A black brittle star is hiding in a grove of a red sponge. The water current produced by the sponge carries nutrients to the brittle stars.
Photo: G.S. Lewbel.

Worthy of a movie set, the wreck of a small tugboat sits upright on a white sand bottom in less than 20 feet (6 meters) of water. Photo: L. R. Martin.

All of the location and street names used in this book are spelled to conform to the Shell Curaçao Road Map ("Mapa di Kaya"). The Shell map is the only decent, detailed map available for Curaçao. If you rent a car or plan to do any shore diving, the Shell map will be invaluable. Even if you don't drive around, the Shell map will be useful to pinpoint dive sites described in this book, although the dive operators know them by name. You can buy Shell map at most hotels and gas stations.

Seaquarium. Even seasoned divers will enjoy a visit to the Seaquarium. A new facility located at Bapor Kibra just past the Princess Beach Hotel and Casino, it boasts a spectacular collection of invertebrates and fishes. A tour of the Seaquarium is one of the best ways to learn the Caribbean fauna, since you won't be limited by bottom time, and most tanks are well-labeled. Admission is about $5 for adults. At the time of this writing an amusement park with water slides was under construction, in case you have to sit out a dive and still want to get wet.

2

Diving on Curaçao

This book describes a number of dive locations on Curaçao. Some are accessible only by boat, and others are accessible from shore. Although not every dive site has been included, this book will guide you to some of the best sites.

The southwest shore is more amenable to diving, and most of the diving takes place on that side of the island. The Curaçao Underwater Park stretches eastward from Willemstad, along the eastern end (Oostpunt) of the southwest shore. The Park and the eastern end of the southwest shore are exposed to more heavy weather than is the western end (Westpunt) of the southwest shore. You are strongly encouraged to buy the Guide to the Curaçao Underwater Park, produced by the Netherlands Antilles National Parks Foundation, if you plan to dive in the Park.

This books includes sites in the Park—which can be dived year-round, but is much calmer during fall and early winter—and in the area of the west of Willemstad, which tends to be calm year-round.

Drop-offs. Much of the diving on Curaçao is near gradual drop-offs, but some of the drop-offs are sheer vertical walls. Although most drop-offs begin at a depth of 30–40 feet (9–12 meters), they often extend beyond safe limits for sport diving. Nearly all sites have good shallow-water diving inshore of the drop-offs.

Except for occasionally rough water on the surface in some areas, there are not likely to be any water conditions requiring special techniques for sport divers at most sites mentioned in this guide. Currents are generally minimal (less than $\frac{1}{4}$ knot) at most of these sites. The drop-offs may have currents (mostly parallel to shore), but drift diving has not yet come to Curaçao. If there's some current at a dive site, either be sure that you can make reasonable progress against it or get out of the water. Remember to begin your dive against the direction of flow so that you can get back to the boat easily if you tire.

A bright orange basket sponge dominates the sloping drop-off at Piedra di Sombre. Photo: L. R. Martin.

Curaçao is a relatively long, narrow island and may be thought of conveniently as having two sides: a windward shore facing northeast and a leeward shore facing southwest. The northeast shore is rarely dived by visitors, though a few brave locals have their favorite secret spots there. The water is almost always rough on the northeast side of the island, which takes the full brunt of waves driven more or less continually by the tradewinds. Seen from the air, the northeast shore is often white with breaking waves. Sites on the northeast shore are not included in this guide due to difficulty of access and typically dangerous water conditions.

Wet suits and gloves are strongly recommended for all shore dives. Ironshore can shred your feet and hands. For shore dives, be sure not to swim farther than your capabilities allow for a safe, easy return. For shore diving in particular, novices should be sure that another diver with advanced training is present to help evaluate water conditions. You should also take along a dive flag on a float. Before your dive, arrange with someone on shore to keep watch and to meet you at your exit point at a given time. That way, if you have problems, help can be summoned promptly. Be sure to lock your valuables securely in your car, too.

Curaçao is rapidly becoming a diver-oriented island, although diving tourism on Curaçao is still fairly undeveloped compared to Bonaire or Grand Cayman. Consider this: the diving is outstanding—as good as we've seen anywhere in the Caribbean—and it's mostly virgin or near-virgin diving.

Services. Curaçao has excellent diving services. You can rent tanks and get good fills; you can rent gear if you don't bring your own; and you can set up complete packages with competent dive operators who can handle your boat or shore needs. You may have to do a bit more work to arrange it than you would in a place that is used to 1,000 divers every month, and the water conditions may not be perfect at every location for 365 days a year. Because Curaçao is an island, however, there's always a lee side where the diving will be good on almost any day.

Instruction. Until the mid-1980's, Curaçao was a prime destination for experienced divers and a less-than-ideal destination for novices. That has all changed in the last two years, as dive operators realized the economic benefits of reaching the American dive travel market. These days, nearly all the dive operators on Curaçao have employed certified, English-speaking diving instructors in an effort to meet the needs of tourists and divers wanting additional training.

Nearly all of the instructors on Curaçao have been certified by American training agencies, and offer introductory-level through advanced and specialty courses. If you need training, be sure to set it up in advance with the dive operator you choose, and don't be afraid to ask to see an instructor's certification card. The certified instructors on the island are generally excellent, and are proud of their training. There are a few dive guides who teach scuba (i.e. uncertified instructors) on Curaçao, but competition is very likely to force them into instructors' courses in the near future.

Most operators send qualified divemasters out on their boats if instructors are not required. These instructors, divemasters and store-employed dive guides are a good source of information regarding water conditions on Curaçao, and should be consulted before diving any of the shore sites described in this book.

Gorgonians are most abundant on shallow shelves above drop-offs. Photo: L. R. Martin.

Air Stations. There is one reliable air filling station easily accessible to divers at the time of this writing (June 1988): Masterdive's facility at the Seaquarium (phone 616666). In a pinch, you can obtain fills from the Curaçao Oxigen Co., in the Konigsplein area north of the Amstel Brewery. Phone 76777, and ask for directions.

The other dive operators on the island usually have full tanks available for rent, although most of them do not have compressors and buy their air from Masterdive. Sometimes—especially late in the day—you'll be unable to rent a full tank from them unless you have made the necessary arrangements in advance. If you plan ahead, they'll reserve tanks for you.

Make sure you pick up your tanks during normal business hours. The dive operators are not usually open at night, and if you have a late or early morning shore dive planned, you'll have to get your tanks before they shut down at the end of the day.

Dive Operators. A list of current phone numbers and addresses for dive operators on Curaçao is provided in Appendix 1. There is one retail sales operations on Curacao: Masterdive located at the Seaquarium. It has a very complete selection of diving equipment for sale and rent. Underwater photo and video gear is available, and various regulators and other equipment can be serviced or repaired by Masterdive.

Gear rental can be arranged through any dive operator on the island. Most of the equipment for rent is purchased from American manufacturers, meaning that you'll have access to an assortment of brands available in the States. Nearly all of the tanks on the island are aluminum 80's, although some operators keep a few steels on hand for oldtimers.

Guided boat dives are offered by Piscadera Watersports at the Curaçao Caribbean, Coral Cliff Diving at the Coral Cliff Resort & Beach Club, Underwater Curaçao at the Seaquarium, and Dive Curaçao & Watersports at the Princess Beach Hotel. The operators usually prefer sites near their facilities, since Curaçao is a large island and the running time to distant sites would be expensive. Furthermore, rough water offshore is common, and the shorter the ride, the better.

Coral Cliff Diving is the only operator routinely visiting the sites near the west end of the island, between Rif (Kaap St. Marie) and Westpunt. Piscadera Watersports usually serves the area between Rif and Willemstad, in the center of the southwest coast of Curaçao. Underwater Curaçao, and Dive Curaçao & Watersports mainly dive in the Curaçao Underwater Park, between Willemstad and the eastern end of Curaçao (Oostpunt).

A wide variety of seaworthy dive boats is available on the island, and operators tend to use whatever boat fits the group they have on any given day. If you're by yourself, or with only a few people, you'll probably take a small, open outboard-powered boat. If you're part of a larger group, you'll probably have the use of a larger, custom dive boat. At the end of your dive, you'll find showers, rinse barrels, and all the usual amenities.

Branching brown sponge on the drop-off. Photo: G. S. Lewbel.

Dive Sites

Snorkeling. The symbol * indicates that the site includes areas that are good for snorkelers as well as scuba divers. Many sites are adjacent to drop-offs or walls which extend beyond sport diving depths; where this is the case, the indication of the typical depth range includes the notation "unlimited".

The Dive Sites. Due to the drop-offs and drastic depths, a rating chart for most dive sites is not possible. Novice and intermediate divers should be accompanied by a qualified divemaster or instructor when diving on or near walls or steep drop-offs. Location names within the Curaçao Underwater Park conform to those in the "Guide to the Curaçao Underwater Park" by Tom van't Hof and Heleen Cornet; those outside the Park conform to the Shell Road Map of Curaçao. Buoy numbers are those used by the Park, which proceed in sequence from west to east.

Large stands of elkhorn coral grow in the shallow water of Piedra Pretu. Photo L.R. Martin.

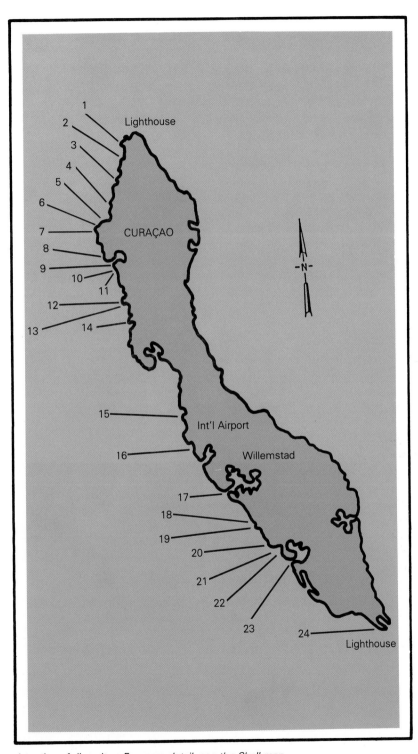

1

2

3

4

5

6

7

8

9

10

11

12

13

14

15

16

17

18

19

20

21

22

23

24

Lighthouse

CURAÇAO

Int'l Airport

Willemstad

Lighthouse

-N-

Location of dive sites. For more detail, see the Shell map.

Typical depth range	:	20 feet (6 meters) to unlimited
Access	:	Shore or boat

Playa Kalki is located at the northwestern end of Curaçao, and can be reached by boat or by car. If you're in a car, drive to the village called the Dorp Westpunt, turn off the main highway at the cemetery, take an immediate left turn at the end of the cemetery, follow the road until you come to a "T", left again a few hundred feet to the head of the concrete stairs, and you're there. You'll find the name of the beach written in coral pieces embedded in the concrete steps leading to the water. It's easier to find than it sounds, and it's well worth the trip. The drive to the tip of the island is beautiful, but the dive offers some really unusual underwater scenery.

Snorkeling. Playa Kalki is a well-sheltered cove that is calm nearly all the time. You can gear up in the parking lot (be sure to lock your valuables securely), hike down the steps, and dive from the white sand beach. The nearshore coral offers good snorkeling and clear water. Farther offshore, the bottom slopes very gradually downward, in most places at less than 20°. The shallower portions of this area are suitable for novices, since the slope is as gentle as it is on most shelves or terraces above drop-offs in other locations.

High-voltage fish action may be expected at this site. Photo: G.S. Lewbel.

A white mist anemone (Heteractis lucida) *withdraws into a crevice in a star coral boulder. Photo: L. R. Martin.*

The site is also perfect for training, since you can select any depth range you wish and stay within it easily. In most places, there is not really any crest, just a smooth transition from shallow to deeper water. The view down-slope from about 30 feet (9 meters) resembles rolling hills seen from a mountain top. Nearly every surface you see is completely covered with living coral. Toward the center of the cove, you'll find compact mounds of star coral forming little Hobbit-like villages at depths of about 60 feet (18 meters). You can also see great piles of sheet or plate coral in deeper water, below 100 feet (30 meters).

Gorgonians line the crest of the drop-off at Playa Kalki. Photo: L. R. Martin.

Knipbaai* and Sweet Alice 2

Typical depth range   :   40 feet (12 meters) to unlimited
Access   :   Shore (Knipbaai) and boat (Sweet
                                  Alice)

Knipbaai is a cove similar to Playa Jeremi, but about three times wider. It is an excellent beach dive, though it requires substantially more swimming to get to coral. For this reason, it is often dived by boat. The areas between Knipbaai and Playa Jeremi called Sweet Alice is accessible only by boat, and has the best-developed coral. Knipbaai is located between Playa Jeremi and Playa Abao (also called Big Knip). Sweet Alice lies near the edge of the drop-off in water about 60 feet deep. The drop-off falls off sharply to over 130 feet. The lip of the drop-off is densely covered with large coral heads and gorgonians. Shallower portions of Knipbaai may be dived easily by novices, but the drop-off begins in fairly deep water and is for intermediate and advanced divers only.

Queen conchs (Strombus gigas) *are abundant in the shallower, sandy portions of Knipbaai. Photo: G. S. Lewbel.*

To dive Knipbaai from the beach, turn westward from the main road between Dorp Lagun and Knip at the small green-and-white sign to Knipbaai. You'll come immediately to a toll booth (usually abandoned), and then to a fork in the road. Bear left at the fork to get to Playa Jeremi. There is a shady parking lot and a white sand beach. It is protected from weather, and calm seas and little or no current may be expected much of the time.

The easiest entry and exit is on the sandy south side of the beach. Stay close to the south wall of the cove. En route, you'll find gorgonians up to 8 feet high, conchs on the sand, and small caverns in the wall that are filled with copper and glassy sweepers. If it's calm on the surface, you may notice the mixing of salt and fresh water from these caverns causing a shimmering effect. Near the surface along the wall, you'll also see orange cup corals. Swim seaward within sight of the wall until you get to the coral. Snorkelers will find the best scenery along this wall near the beach and in the center of the cove just outside the surf line.

Heavy coral cover starts in water of 40–50 feet deep, near the wide mouth of the cove. It's a 15-minute swim, so you may want to stay on the surface on the way out, then work your way back in on the bottom at the end of the dive. Just before you leave the water, take a look at the long rocky shallow ledge parallel to the beach in the middle of the cove. It's in less than 6 feet of water. There are usually schools of sweepers under the ledge, milling balls of fingerlings, big morays, and needlefish working the surface next to the ledge.

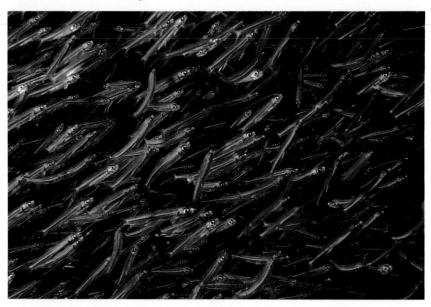

Fingerlings under the ledge in the center of Knipbaai, near the beach, may be seen by snorkelers. Photo: G. S. Lewbel.

A feather duster worm (Sabellastarte magnifica) *and a giant Caribbean anemone* (Condylactis gigantea) *sharing space in a mountainous star coral* (Montastrea annularis), *along with Christmas tree worms* (Spirobranchus giganteus) *and cleaner shrimps* (Periclimenes sp.). *Photo: G. S. Lewbel.*

33

Typical depth range	:	40 feet (12 meters) to unlimited
Access	:	Shore

Playa Jeremi is a beautiful little cove on the road south of Knipbaai. It is best dived from the beach. You'll see the turnoff on the road between Dorp Lagun and Knip marked by a small green and white sign. There is a small parking area and a short trail to the beach. The beach is smooth, offering a perfect entry and exit. The cove is protected from most weather, and is usually glassy calm. Playa Jeremi is an ideal location for a night dive.

In the center of the cove, the sandy bottom has many burrowing urchins, conchs, lizardfishes, goatfish, and peacock flounders. To get to the coral, swim over the sand westward to the mouth of the cove. The swim takes 5–10 minutes. The center of the cove is a bit deeper than the edges. Corals starts at about 30–40 feet near the edges of the cove, and between 40 feet and 50 feet in the center. The farther out you go, the better the coral gets. Particularly noteworthy are some extremely large heads of mountainous star coral.

Stinging carpet anemone (Lebrunnea danae) *have powerful stinging cells, and should not be touched with bare skin. Photo: G. S. Lewbel.*

Orange cup corals (Tubastrea aurea) *are at their best at night along the sides of the cove at Playa Jeremi. Photo: G. S. Lewbel.*

35

On the way back from the dive, stay close to the left (north) wall of the cove facing the beach. You'll see a very large rock sticking out of the water. The rock has a rickety wooden ladder on it. Snorkelers will want to head directly for the rock too. The wall and the rock are covered with orange cup corals. Large trumpet fish hang out next to the wall, along with glassy sweepers and copper sweepers beneath ledges. Photographers will want both wide-angle and macro gear for this dive.

A sponge in deeper water growing on an agariciid plate coral. Photo: G. S. Lewbel.

Playa Lagun* 4

Typical depth range	:	30 feet (9 meters) to unlimited
Access	:	Shore or boat

Playa Lagun is just south of the town of Lagun on the coastal road. It has a very small bay and a sandy beach on which fishing boats are usually drawn up. It can be dived by boat but is perfect for a shore dive because of its easy entry and exit, calm water, and nearby drop-off. It is sheltered from weather and remains nearly flat all the time.

Good Snorkeling. There is good snorkeling along the base of the cliffs that line both sides of the bay, and a drop-off just a short swim offshore. The drop-off begins at a depth of 30–40 feet (9–12 meters) and slopes downward at about 45° to beyond sport diving range. The center of the bay has a mixture of sand and coral, but the drop-off is fairly solid coral from the lip on down. It's almost a picture-postcard location for training dives. You can drive to within 25 feet (8 meters) of the water, gear up in the shade of trees on the shore, and buy a cold drink from a shop by the beach when you get back out.

A huge, eroded stand of mountainous star coral (Montastrea annularis) *stands out from the lip of the drop-off. The recesses in such undercut formations often harbor small tropicals such as royal grammas. Photo: L. R. Martin.*

To get there by car, turn off the main road at Dorp Lagun (between Dorp Westpunt and Dorp Soto). The turnoff point is marked by a sign to Playa Lagun. If you're going north, it's a left turn into the parking lot. Another landmark to watch for from the main road is a concrete construction site fenced with barbed wire in the parking lot.

Open fishing boats, such as these, are in daily use in Curaçao. No boat is needed to dive Playa Lagun, however. Good snorkeling is available at the base of the cliffs, and the drop-off is just a short swim away. Photo: L. R. Martin.

Mushroom Forest 5

Typical depth range	:	30–40 feet (9–12 meters)
Access	:	Boat

Mushrooom Forest is just to the north of Sponge Forest, between Boca Santa Cruz and Boca Santu Pretu. It is sheltered from wind and waves under typical conditions. The surface is usually calm, and there are generally no significant currents. Although Mushroom Forest is near Playa Chikitu, public access to the beach is restricted. Mushroom Forest is up on the shallow shelf inshore of the deeper slope, and is an excellent dive for novices. Advanced divers won't be bored here, though.

Spiny lobsters (Panulirus argus) *hide under coral heads at Mushroom Forest. Photo: G. S. Lewbel.*

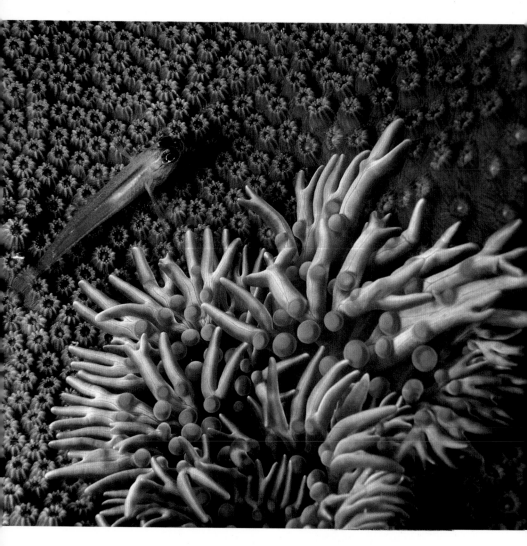

Stinging carpet anemones (Lebrunnea danae) *and a peppermint goby* (Coryphopterus lipernes) *share space on a mountainous star coral* (Montastrea annularis) *at Mushroom Forest. Photo: G. S. Lewbel.*

Diverse Site. Mushroom Forest is one of the most complex dive sites in the Caribbean, despite its relatively flat profile. The diversity is astonishing. Everywhere you look, you'll see something new. This is a great location to use one of the waterproof guides to fish and corals. Many of the coral heads are eroded with small holes and tunnels through and between them. Lots of lobsters, spotted drums, spotted morays, green morays, and chain morays call Mushroom Forest home. If you're trying to learn the anemones of the Caribbean, take a good look at the cracks in the coral at Mushroom Forest. A bit of searching will reveal nearly every species.

Mountainous star corals (Montastrea aonularis) *form beautiful mounds at Mushroom Forest. Photo: G. S. Lewbel.*

Typical depth range   :   40–60 feet (12–18 meters)
Access   :   Boat

Marlon's Mystery Spot is just to the southwest and seaward of the Mushroom Forest on the shelf next to the slope. It is frequently swept by currents. It should, therefore, be visited only by advanced divers used to turbulent conditions.

There is a very wide shelf on the inner edge of the site. The shelf has several nice stands of pillar coral, many spotted drums, huge gorgonians and basket sponges, and an excellent assortment of anemones.

Intense Fish Action. The fish above the shelf provide most of the action. Blue and brown chromis form enormous schools to feed on plankton in the current. In addition, you can often see dozens of trumpet-fish darting around in the water and feeding on smaller fishes, rather than skulking along the bottom in their usual fashion. Herds of parrotfish swim along as if they were on paths, and aggressive damselfishes will help to remind divers about their buoyancy control.

Seaward of the site, a slope begins in about 60 feet, falls off to several sandy terraces, and then drops into very deep water. The slope is fairly featureless by comparison to others described in this book, and probably not worth the residual nitrogen you'd build up there on a deep dive.

Blue chromis (Chromis cyaneus) *meet head-on above the coral in a territorial mating display. Photo: G.S. Lewbel.*

Bright yellow sponges extend upward into the current filtering out tiny particles of food. Photo: G. S. Lewbel.

Typical depth range	:	40 feet (12 meters) to unlimited
Access	:	Boat

Sponge Forest lies to the northwest of Franklin's Special off Boca Hulu. It is accessible only by boat. Because it is somewhat protected by a point of land to the southeast of Boca Hulu, water conditions are usually fairly calm here, and current velocity is usually low.

The shelf near shore is about 20 feet deep. It has many fine small brain corals on it, though it is a bit sandier than the shelves at Franklin's Special and the Mushroom Forest. For this reason, it's not as interesting a shallow dive, but the slope below it is well worth a trip. The slope begins at about

A bicolor damselfish (Pomacentrus partitus) *faces off a queen parrotfish* (Scarus vetula) *and wins the battle of wills. Photo: G. S. Lewbel.*

Clusters of basket sponges (Xestospongia muta) *distinguish Sponge Forest. Photo:*
G. S. Lewbel.

40 feet and drops gradually to a sandy base at around 130 feet. Upper portions of the slope are suitable for supervised novices and intermediate divers, while deeper portions should be the province of advanced divers only.

Huge Basket and Branched Sponges. There are a number of very large basket sponges (some over 6 feet high) on deeper parts of the slope at Sponge Forest. Even more abundant are the large, branched sponges that form tangled nests of brown and purple fingers over 10 feet across. Photographers will want to take wide-angle lenses to Sponge Forest for shots of these unusual formations.

Typical depth range   :   30 feet (9 meters) to unlimited
Access   :   Boat

Franklin's Special is located approximately 10 minutes' boat ride to the north of the mouth of Santa Martabaai, between Boca Pos Spano and Boca Santa Marta. It can be dived only by boat. The small sandy beach to the west of Franklin's Special is not accessible to the public. Current velocity is usually fairly low, and currents generally run from east to west, parallel to shore. There is a shallow reef crest at about 30 feet, and then the slope falls off more-or-less gradually into deeper water, with heavy coral cover down to about 130 feet in most places. Below the coral is a sandy white bottom, and the slope decreases in steepness. The shelf is suitable for novices, while the upper portions of the slope may be dived safely by supervised novices as a result of its fairly gentle angle of incline.

Intermediate and advanced divers will find the slope of Franklin's Special an excellent site for deeper dives. It has many very large colonies of black coral and dense populations of feather duster worms. Trumpetfish and queen angels favor the site, and it would be unusual not to see a dozen or more on a single dive. Photographers may prefer macro setups at this location, due to the rather uniform topography.

Queen angelfish (Holacanthus ciliaris) *poses for a close shot at Franklin's Special.*
Photo: G. S. Lewbel.

Trumpetfish (Aulostomus maculatus) *often sneak up on smaller fishes by pretending they're gorgonians. Photo: G. S. Lewbel.*

French angelfishes (Pomacanthus paru) *are common on the shelf at Hell's Corner.*
Photo: G. S. Boland.

Antipatharian wire corals 8' long project into the current along the drop-off in water
deeper than 100'. Photo: G. S. Boland.

| **Typical depth range** | : | 30 feet (9 meters) to unlimited |
| **Access** | : | Boat |

Hell's Corner is immediately to the west of the mouth of Santa Martabaai. Although it is sometimes calm, water conditions on the surface are usually quite rough, and high-velocity currents from surface to bottom are typical. Hell's Corner should therefore be dived only by advanced divers with experience in turbulent water and strong currents. The current usually runs from east to west, approximately parallel to shore, but large eddies are not uncommon since the site lies near a point of land that projects outward from shore. If you should get into trouble, there is a sandy beach just to the north of Hell's Corner that might serve as an emergency exit. From the beach, it's a short hike to the Coral Cliff and Santa Martabaai.

Hell's corner has a shallow shelf that breaks at about 30 feet, and then falls off gradually at a 45° angle or greater to depths of about 130 feet. Below this, the angle of the slope decreases somewhat. Coral covers the upper reaches of the slope. The site is frequently visited by large pelagic fish, and sea turtles are often seen there. Gorgonians up to 8 feet in height wave in the current. Photographers will probably do best with a wide-angle lens at Hell's Corner. Although there are plenty of small subjects, shooting macro in a 3-knot current may be challenging, to say at least.

Typical depth range	:	10–20 feet (3–6 meters)
Access	:	Shore

Wet Suit City is a shallow beach dive directly in front of the Coral Cliff Resort & Beach Club. The site is exposed to waves, and should not be dived except under fairly calm conditions. The dive is suitable for novices, and fun for snorkelers. You'll want boots, a full suit, and a pair of gloves to protect you from the main feature of the site: fire coral.

To dive Wet Suit City, go down the paved driveway at the hotel, turn left, and enter the water at the sandy spot just to the left of left-hand breakwater (facing the sea). Swim out to water 10 feet deep, and turn left parallel to shore. Be careful to stay over the sand until you're in water deep enough for swimming; there are small coral heads in the surf line to either side of the sand patch. You can exit at the same spot, or through the passageway between the two breakwaters and into the lagoon.

Extensive Fire Coral. Wet Suit City is a very interesting dive for macro-photographers. Its beautiful stands of fire coral form delicate sheets and plates up to 3 feet high. Extra care is required here to avoid damaging the site, since the fire coral is fragile, and there is usually some surge from waves. You will find many bristle worms (also called fire worms, with good reason) at Wet Suit City, some up to a foot long. The fire coral also shelters schools of tiny juvenile brown chromis.

Sharknose gobies (Gobiosoma evelynae) *are usually found on corals rather than sponges, and clean fishes for a living. Photo: G. S. Lewbel.*

Tentacles of an anemone reach out into the current to filter drifting nutrients. Photo L.R. Martin.

Spotlight gobies (Gobiosoma louisae) *are usually found on sponges, often eating parasitic worms that infest the sponges. Photo: G. S. Lewbel.*

Large gorgonian fans (Gorgonia ventalina *and* G. flabellum) *usually have their blades oriented perpendicular to the current or average direction of wave motion. Photo: G. S. Lewbel.*

Typical depth range : 40 feet (12 meters) to unlimited
Access : Shore

The Coral Cliff Drop-off is located in front of the Coral Cliff Resort & Beach Club, near the mouth of Santa Martabaai. The entry and exits are as described for Wet Suit City. It is not uncommon to have some current at the Coral Cliff drop-off, as well as some surface chop. The current typically runs parallel to shore and toward the northwest. The dive is most suitable for intermediate and advanced divers, though supervised novices can safely dive the upper portions of the slope on calm days.

The best part of the drop-off is about five minutes' swim to the southeast (left, facing the sea) of Wet Suit City. To dive the drop-off, cross Wet Suit City and then turn seaward to the edge of the shelf. Proceed along the lip until the coral looks good, and then descend. The drop-off begins about 40 feet deep, and falls off gently to a series of terraces at about 60 feet, and then slopes steeply toward a white sand bottom below 100 feet.

Garden Eel Colonies. Some of the terraces and the area at the base of the drop-off have garden eel colonies on them. The drop-off has fair coral cover, though there are large sandy areas between coral heads. There are few large basket sponges, but many smaller loggerhead and vase sponges up to 2 feet across, and some very impressive gorgonian fans.

Typical depth range	:	30–60 feet (9–18 meters)
Access	:	Boat or Shore

Inner San Juan lies north of Outer San Juan, between Playa Mansalina and Boca Grandi, within sight of San Juanbaai. It is accessible by boat or from the beach. To reach it from shore, turn southwest off the main road between Dorp Sint Willibrordus and Dorp Soto at the small sign marking Landhuis San Juan. The turnoff is just north of the road to Dokterstuin.

Follow the road past the large Landhuis, take the second turn to the left, and follow it to the water. The road past Landhuis San Juan is private, and there is usually an admission charge of about $3 per car. There are two beaches next to one another. The larger beach to the north (right side, facing the water) has less coral rubble and is a better entry and exit spot. There is plenty of shady parking there.

From the beach, it is less then five minutes' swim over sand to the start of the coral. Coral cover increases with depth, and by the time the water is 50 feet deep, you'll see high-relief star coral heads the size of small houses. The bottom is relatively flat in most places and slopes gently into deeper water. There are many crevices and holes eroded beneath the huge coral heads, often inhabited by eels, spotted drums, and lobsters. Due to the gentleness of the slope, shallower portions of the site can be dived by novices.

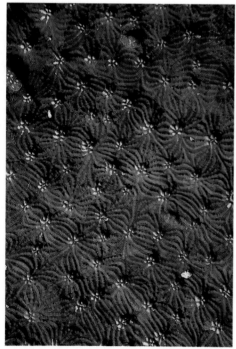

A fungus coral (Mycetophyllia aliciae) *spreads out in deep water to catch light, its white dots marking the colony's multiple mouths. Photo: G. S. Lewbel.*

Creole wrasses (Clepticus parrai) *are groomed by a juvenile Spanish hogfish* (Bodianus rufus) *at a cleaning station. Photo: G. S. Lewbel.*

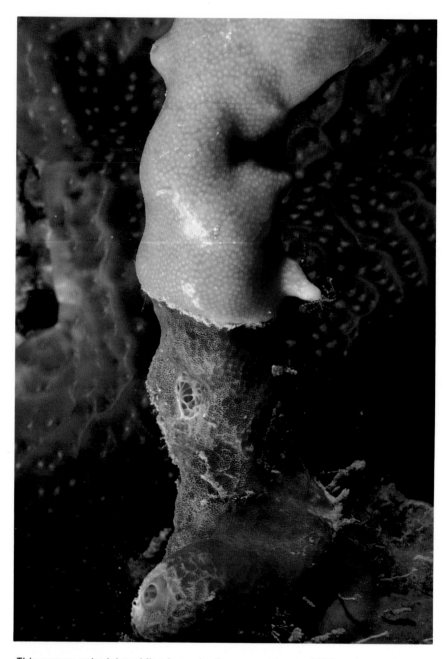

This orange colonial ascidian is gradually overgrowing and killing the purple sponge, using the sponge's fibrous skeleton as a structural support.
Photo: G.S. Lewbel.

Typical depth range : 20–50 feet (6–15 meters)

Access : Boat

Outer San Juan is located on the northwest side of Punt Halve Dag, just south of Playa Mansalina. Since it is protected by Punt Halve Dag, conditions are usually calm, and little or no current is typical. Outer San Juan is located on a shallow shelf adjacent to a coral-covered, sloping drop-off that falls more-or-less steeply to a sandy bottom below 100 feet. The site is suitable for novices, so long as they stay away from the nearby slope.

Butterprint Brain Corals. The broad shelf is distinguished by beautiful heads of butterprint brain coral. There are also many medium-sized and large basket sponges, and good coral cover. Due to its proximity to Inner San Juan—a great place for a deep dive—Outer San Juan is an excellent place for a repetitive or shallow dive. You'll probably enjoy the shelf at Outer San Juan more than the drop-off next to it. The outer edge of the shelf ranges from about 20 to about 50 feet deep. Although it offers decent deep diving, the drop-off is not spectacular compared to others (such as Cas Abao and Playa Kalki) described in this book.

Butterprint brain corals (Meandrina meandrites) *are one of the most distinctive features of the shelf at Outer San Juan. Photo: G. S. Lewbel.*

Typical depth range	:	30 feet (9 meters) to unlimited
Access	:	Boat

Cas Abao is located off the beach of Play'i Shon, near the center of Valentijnsbaai, and to the southeast of Punt Halve Dag. It is accessible only by boat, as the roads to the beach are not open to the public. The dive site is protected from the prevailing winds by a point of land to the south, and generally has calm conditions and fairly little current.

Cas Abao has a shallow shelf near shore with a lip at about 25 feet. Beneath this lip, the coral-covered slope falls off sharply to a white sand bottom below 140 feet. The slope is incredibly rich in marine life, especially in the crevices beneath coral heads. You can often see lobsters there, and it would not be unusual to find several spotted drums together under a single coral head. Toward the deeper parts of the slope, brilliant orange elephant-ear sponges 3 feet high project upward. The shelf is suitable for novices, but the slope is steep in many areas and should be dived by intermediate and advanced divers only.

Spotted drums (Equetus punctatus) *can be found near the bases of coral heads on almost any visit to Cas Abao. Photo: G. S. Lewbel.*

A giant Caribbean anemone (Condylactis gigantea) *in an orange sponge at Cas Abao. Photo: G. S. Lewbel.*

Typical depth range	:	30 feet (9 meters) to unlimited
Access	:	Shore or boat

Vaersenbaai is between Dorp Sint Michiel and Bullenbaai, northwest of Willemstad. It can be dived by boat, of course, but the real attraction of Vaersenbaai is that it's an ideal spot for shore training. It is maintained as a weekend retreat for island police officers, and is clean and well kept. There is a concrete parking lot, benches and picnic facilities, and a short pier with steps right into the water. These features make it a popular site with the locals for night diving too. If you're with a group or class and want a place to gear up without getting sandy, a no-hassle entry and exit, predictably perfect water conditions, and a short swim to a drop-off, Vaersenbaai is right for you. It's about 5 miles (8 kilometers) northwest of Willemstad, on the road to Bullenbaai and Meiber; just look for the sign to Vaersenbaai on your left.

Vaersenbaai is a protected location and is nearly always calm. It's therefore a good bet when the Curacao Underwater Park is too rough to dive. The drop-off can be seen easily from the beach, since it's only about five minutes' swim away. On the way to the drop-off, there are coral heads that will interest snorkelers. The drop-off is comparable to most of the other drop-offs on the island, cresting at about 30–40 feet (9–12 meters) and sloping downward at about 45° in most places to depths exceeding 100 feet (30 meters).

Yellow goatfish (Mulloidichthys martinicus) *working the shallows. Photo: G. S. Lewbel.*

Three different sponges blend in a spectacular array of colors. Photo: G. S. Lewbel.

Snorkelers can enter Blauwbaai from the sandy beach, while divers for the drop-off find the shore entry near the outside of the bay closer to the wall. Photo: L. R. Martin.

Blauwbaai* 16

Typical depth range	:	30 feet (9 meters) to unlimited
Access	:	Boat or shore

Blauwbaai (Blue Bay) is a sheltered cove between Piscaderabaai and the town of Dorp Sint Michiel. The bay has a sandy beach, picnic facilities, bathrooms, and a small sundries shop. You'll have no trouble finding it on the Shell map of Curaçao. There is a fee of a couple of dollars for entry, but tourists are sometimes exempted from the fee as an act of goodwill. Less than 5 miles (8 kilometers) from Willemstad, it is a popular weekend beach with locals. The bay is also a good spot for a boat dive offering a protected anchorage and a very pretty drop-off.

If you plan to dive Blauwbaai from the beach, you'll find good snorkeling to either side of the bay entrance along the rocks. The center of the bay is fairly sandy and suitable for training, but not big on scenery. The drop-off at the outer edge of the bay is within swimming distance of the shore, but it's a long way from the sandy beach by the parking lot. Rather than enter at the sandy beach in the center of the bay if you're going to the drop-off, drive around to the left side of the mouth of the bay (facing the water), just beyond a large pile of concrete rubble and short of a series of very large boulders. The small beach here is within 5 minutes' swim of the lip of the drop-off.

Colonian zoanthid anemones (Palythoa caribaeorum) *form thick rubbery mats on the wreck of the S.S. Oranje Nassau. Photo: G.S. Lewbel.*

Steep Drop-off. The drop-off at Blauwbaai has a lip at about 30 feet (9 meters) and falls off steeply to depths exceeding 150 feet (46 meters). In some places the drop-off is nearly vertical, but in most areas it is closer to 45°. There are many sheet coral, black coral, wire coral, and sponges on the drop-off. If you're making the transition between diving on slopes and diving on vertical walls, Blauwbaai is an excellent place for training.

Yellow pencil coral and brain coral live side by side on the drop-off at Blauwbaai. Photo L.R. Martin.

Large mounds of butterprint brain coral (Meandrina meandrites) *dominate many of Curacao's dive sites. Photo: G.S. Lewbel.*

Typical depth range	:	40–110 feet (27–34 meters)
Access	:	Boat or shore

The *Superior Producer* is a sunken coastal freighter that rests upright and completely intact on a sand bottom at about 110 feet (34 meters). In 1977, the ship was outward bound from St. Anna Baai heavily overloaded with a cargo of clothing. After leaving the harbor entrance and turning west, it filled with water and sank within a stone's throw of shore just west of Rif Stadium, the old baseball and soccer field. The top of the wheelhouse is about 80 feet (25 meters) deep, and the bridge is about 90 feet (27 meters) deep, so this dive is for advanced divers only.

The wreck is still fairly clean of marine life, although anemones and corals have started to grow on it. If you want some shots of yourself on the bridge of a large ship, or waving over the railing to the crowds, bring your wide-angle lens and your strobe. The white ceramic toilet in the room next to the bridge suggests some shots too. Local divers got all the really good stuff almost immediately after the ship sank. The cargo and the brass must have been quite valuable; the local divers gave the recompression chamber in Willemstad plenty of business. It's deep, so be careful to watch your bottom time.

You can dive the *Superior Producer* from the shore, although it's better on most days to dive from a boat. The site is exposed to wave action, and you'll run a gauntlet of coral heads and urchins all the way to the beach. If you have a very calm day and heavy boots and gloves, you might give it a try. Drive along the shore in front of the old ball park on Gouv. Van Slobbeweg until you come to a big cement block on the beach. The road dead-ends going west; the block is a few hundred yards from the end. You'll then be able to see the mooring buoy for the *Superior Producer* a short distance offshore. Swim to the buoy, head down the cable to the bottom, and then straight out for a short swim to the freighter.

Though a young wreck, the Superior Producer *has attracted a few anemones and other attaching marine organisms. Photo: L. R. Martin.*

Loaded with clothing when it went down in 1977, the freighter bottomed out at 110 feet (34 meters). Though a deep dive, it's sitting upright on a white sand bottom making exploration easy. Photo: L. R. Martin

Typical depth range	:	20 feet (6 meters) to unlimited
Access	:	Shore

The drop-off directly in front of the Princess Beach Hotel is an excellent location for a warmup dive, or for training, or just for the experience of diving on a good drop-off a few minutes' swim from shore. While the shallow shelf inshore of the drop-off might be suitable for novices some of the time, the location is rather exposed, and wave action and currents often make this site suitable for novices only when accompanied by a qualified divemaster or instructor.

The shelf has many large heads of elkhorn coral and thickets of staghorn coral and gorgonians. The crest of the drop-off is located at about 40 feet (12 meters). Below this lip, the drop-off slopes downward at about 45° to at least 120 feet (36 meters), where it crests again and then drops more steeply. The drop-off has many heads of brain coral and leaf coral, and is thoroughly covered with sponges.

Yellow pencil is found along the crest of the wall at Oswaldo's Drop-off, along with schools of brown chromis. Photo L.R. Martin.

The easiest entry and exit for this dive is the concrete steps at the mouth of the entrance channel to the Princess Beach Hotel's protected anchorage. Dive Curaçao and Watersports is the most convenient place to rent tanks for this dive. Be sure to notify the dive shop personnel that you're diving there so they can keep an eye out for you, and stay out of the channel while boats are moving in the area. The drop-off sometimes is washed by currents from left to right as you face seaward, so you should generally begin your dive by swimming offshore and to the left (southeastward) so that you can return downcurrent. Note the alternative exit mentioned for Car Pile, too, in case currents are stronger than expected.

Yellow colonial anemones overgrowing a stalked hydroid colony. Photo: G. S. Lewbel.

Typical depth range	:	70 feet (21 meters) to unlimited
Access	:	Shore

A large tangled mass of old cars and barges sits on the bottom along most of the coral-covered slope of the drop-off in front of the Princess Beach Hotel. The Car Pile is the remains of an experiment in artificial reef construction that was intended to attract fish as well as divers. The cars are heaped on one another, but many are upright and in pretty good condition, considering their present location. You'll recognize some of your old favorite makes from the 1940s in the pile. If you're careful not to get snagged, you can slip down inside some of the cars on top of the pile for a photograph in the driver's seat. This is an excellent spot for wide-angle shots. Don't get beneath any of the cars or barges, and look out for tangled cables and wire on the bottom. Because of its depth, this dive is recommended for supervised intermediates and more experienced divers only.

A group of car and truck bodies, deposited some years ago, has become a favorite with divers, who swim inside the old wrecks. Photo: L. R. Martin.

Though the car bodies are now a uniform gray-green, the marine life attached to them, such as these purple tube sponges, is multi-hued. Photo: L. R. Martin.

For this dive, use the same exit and entry procedure described for Oswaldo's Drop-off. The best way to get to the site is to swim offshore at an angle of about 45° to the right (westward) until you're over the lip of the drop-off. The lip is at about 40 feet (12 meters). Descend on the lip and continue downward to about 70 feet (21 meters), and then proceed farther to the right until you start to see cars. The cars begin at a depth of about 60 feet (18 meters) and continue downward in a gigantic mound to about 130 feet (40 meters).

There is sometimes a current running from left to right (facing the sea), parallel to shore. You don't want to get carried past the pile if the current is strong, so swim straight offshore to the lip, descend, and continue to the right (again, facing the sea) along the 70 foot (21 meter) contour to the pile. On your way back, if you don't want to buck the current, you can exit at a sandy beach past the tennis courts at the west end of the Princess Beach Hotel.

Typical depth range	:	20 feet (6 meters) to unlimited
Access	:	Boat or shore

The buoy for Jan Thiel (Park Buoy #4) is within sight of Playa Jan Thiel, a beautiful sandy beach at the mouth of Jan Thielbaai. The bay is well protected by a breakwater making for easy beach entries and exits. In fact, it looks so much like the perfect beach dive site that it has been used in several films. The beach has picnic facilities, bathrooms, and other amenities. Admission is several dollars a head, but the fee is often waived for tourists. You can reach Playa Jan Thiel by the coast road eastward from the Princess Beach Hotel, or by going west where the road from Bottelier to Caracasbaai dead-ends at the coast.

Club finger coral (Porites porites) *usually looks pink or gray, and has its polyps out in the daytime. Photo: G. S. Lewbel.*

Cleaner shrimp (Periclimenes *sp.*) *near its home base, a pink giant Caribbean anemone* (Condylactis gigantea). *Photo: G. S. Lewbel.*

Good for Novices. The bay is mainly shallow sand and turtle grass 10–20 feet (3–6 meters) high in the middle, and thus of interest for training dives. The sides of the bay have some nice coral heads and gorgonian beds along the shore that will tempt snorkelers. There is a coral-covered shelf between the mouth of the bay and the edge of a gentle drop-off just outside the bay. Areas that will be appropriate for novices include the bay itself and the broad, shallow shelf inshore of the drop-off. The gorgonian and coral bed near the mooring is photogenic, and there's a dense thicket of staghorn coral in shallow water.

The drop-off is typical of those within the park, having lots of star coral, gorgonians, sponges, wire coral, and anemones. It falls off at less than 45° in most places, and could thus be an ideal training site for intermediates. Barrel sponges seem more abundant here than at many other nearby dive sites. The lip of the drop-off is within swimming distance of the beach, but if the water is rough or there are currents present, you might have a difficult time once you get outside the breakwater. Currents toward the northwest are not uncommon on and near the drop-off. If you plan to dive the drop-off, a boat is the most convenient way to go.

Typical depth range	:	20 feet (6 meters) to unlimited
Access	:	Boat

Piedra di Sombré is located between Caracasbaai and Jan Thielbaai. It offers three distinct dives: a stunning vertical wall, a gradual slope, and a shallow terrace. If you plan your dive right, you can see all three areas on a single tank. Facing the sea from the mooring, swim to the edge of the terrace and you'll come to the lip of the wall at a depth of about 30–40 feet (9–12 meters). It is a sheer wall, continuing downward vertically below safe sport diving depths. There are a number of shallow caverns and indentations in the wall, especially in the 70—foot (21—meter) range, where you can see lots of squirrelfish. The wall is covered with wire coral, black coral, star coral and big sponges.

Farther along the wall to the left (facing the sea), the slope becomes less steep and grades into a more gentle slope of about 45°. The slope itself is an excellent dive, having a common crest with the wall and a base that extends below 100 feet (30 meters). It is possible to drop down the wall, track to the southeast on the upward swim, and come up along the slope.

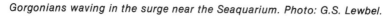

Gorgonians waving in the surge near the Seaquarium. Photo: G.S. Lewbel.

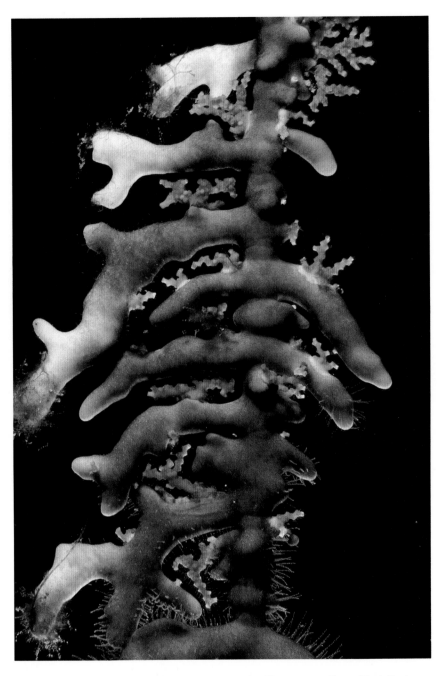

Occasionally, fire coral (Millepora complanata) *will grow together with delicate pink or purple stylasterine coral* (Stylaster roseus). *Photo: G.S. Lewbel.*

A large stand of huge gorgonians and a bed of yellow pencil coral (Madracis mirabilis) *are two of the outstanding features of Piedra di Sombre. Photo: L. R. Martin.*

Giant Gorgonians. The shallow inshore area of the terrace around the cement block that anchors the buoy is ideal for snorkeling and underwater photography. It has a large number of anemones in nooks and crannies and a forest of gorgonians. This forest includes some of the largest gorgonians you are likely to see anywhere (one of these monsters is nearly 8 feet tall!).

Typical depth range	:	15 feet (5 meters) to unlimited
Access	:	Boat

This site is outstanding for photography and offers snorkelers a good look at an intact shipwreck. Towboat (also called Tugboat) is located near the eastern edge of Caracasbaai. The numbered buoy is very near shore, below a collection of petroleum storage tanks and a big orange house on the over-looking cliff. The buoy is somewhat sheltered from prevailing winds, and the site generally is fairly calm. Within a few yards inshore and north of the buoy lies the wreck of a small tugboat, sitting upright on the shelf in less than 20 feet (6 meters) of water. The tugboat is intact, and is generally being overgrown with orange tube coral and other animals and plants. If

Divers can view this small wreck from the inside out; the engine room portholes make excellent frames for an underwater portrait. Photo: L. R. Martin.

Boulders of brain coral cling to the gunwales of the tugboat. A steep drop-off nearby hosts stands of wire coral and black coral. Photo L.R. Martin.

you've used up all your film by the time you get to this wreck, you'll probably want to get back on the boat and reload your camera! You'll also want to get one of your fellow divers to serve as a model for portraits.

Perhaps the best way to dive this site is not to go to the tug directly, but rather to have a look downslope. To the left of the tug (facing seaward) is a beautiful wall starting at about 30 feet (9 meters). The wall is vertical and even undercut in some locations, and extends downward to depths of about 100 feet (30 meters) below, where it takes a more gradual slope of 45° or less. At the base of the wall, there are some very large sheet corals. If you swim slightly to your left facing the wall as you return upslope you'll hit the crest of the wall near the tug, and can swim shoreward a few yards to find the wreck.

Typical depth range	:	20 feet (6 meters) to unlimited
Access	:	Boat

Punt'i Piku is just east of Caracasbaai near the mouth of Spaanse Water (Spanish Water), a large bay used heavily by pleasure boaters. Inshore of the buoy and to the left (facing the sea) is a fine shelf covered with elkhorn and staghorn coral, fire coral, gorgonians, and some very large pillar coral.

Facing seaward, you will find a fairly steep drop-off (over 45°) to the left of the mooring buoy beginning at about 30 feet (9 meters) and continuing to beyond 100 feet (30 meters). The slope is graced by large heads of mountainous star coral at a depth of about 60 feet (18 meters).

Lava-like sheets of mountainous star coral (Montastrea annularis) *drape the edge of the drop-off at Punt'i Piku. Photo: L. R. Martin.*

Vertical Wall. If you're after something even steeper, there is a vertical wall on the other side of the buoy to the right facing seaward. The wall starts at 30–40 feet (9–12 meters) and drops straight down to about 60 feet (18 meters) below, where it slopes off more gently. It is covered with wire coral, gorgonians, and sponges.

Barrel sponges are common in the Curacao Underwater Park. They are long-lived, fragile animals. To avoid them, divers should not handle or bump into them. Photo L.R. Martin.

Typical depth range   :   20 feet (6 meters) to unlimited
Access   :   Boat

Did you ever find a dive spot so good that you didn't want to tell anyone about it? Well, I did, and I'm going to tell you about it. But there's a catch—you may have to pay some heavy dues to get there, and I don't think the location is likely to be dived very often. Piedra Pretu is located at the eastern end of the Curaçao Underwater Park. The nearest operators are about 12 miles (19 kilometers) away. During much of the year, you'll have to ride a boat into heavy chop and high winds for at least an hour before you even see the buoy. Then you'll have to suit up while being bounced around, and you will have another hour's ride home. If you've still got your breakfast in you by the time you get to Buoy #15, however, you're in for a real treat.

While the bright purple tube sponges in the foreground attract attention, the black coral trees silouetted above the diver are much more rare. Black coral is made into semiprecious jewelry in many parts of the world. Photo: L. R. Martin.

Piedra Pretu has the usual shallow terrace above 30 feet (9 meters), suitable for novices. The terrace has staghorn and elkhorn coral and a pretty bed of gorgonians. More experienced divers will want to head for the lip of the wall just to the left (facing seaward) of the mooring buoy. This is one of those spots where you use up all your film in the first five minutes. Piedra Pretu has one of the prettiest vertical walls you're likely to see anywhere in the Caribbean. It runs vertically down to about 120 feet (36 meters), and then slopes off more gradually below that. The wall is covered with a dense forest of black coral. Near the base of the wall, there are big stacked disks of sheet coral the size of table tops. In the 80–90 foot (25–27 meter) depth range, there are crevices going back into the wall, filled with royal grammas and big green moray eels.

Black crinoids are often found perched on gorgonians.
Photo: I.. R. Martin.

Swimming clams (Lima spp.) can swim through the water by opening and closing the two halves of their shells. Most of the time, they live nestled in coral crevices. Photo: G.S. Lewbel.

3

Safety

This chapter discusses common hazards and emergency procedures in case of a diving accident. It does not discuss the diagnosis or treatment of serious medical problems; refer to your first aid manual or emergency diving manual for that information.

Diving is a safe sport and there are very few accidents compared to the number of divers and number of dives made each year. But when the infrequent injury does occur it is necessary to contact medical personnel as rapidly as possible. The telephone numbers and addresses given in this edition were current to the best of the author's knowledge in early 1987. However, the author assumes no responsibility for assuring that phone numbers or contact information are correct. Emergency contact information can change so check on it during or just before the time of your dive trip.

Chamber. In case of a diving accident such as a lung injury or decompression sickness ("bends"), prompt recompression treatment in a chamber may be essential to prevent permanent injury or death.

If you need recompression while in the Netherlands Antilles, I recommend that you get it there rather than attempt to fly to the chambers in the States. Should there be a need for emergency assistance after leaving the Netherlands Antilles—and remember, bends symptoms sometimes don't show up for many hours after a dive and are sometimes brought on by flying—contact DAN immediately.

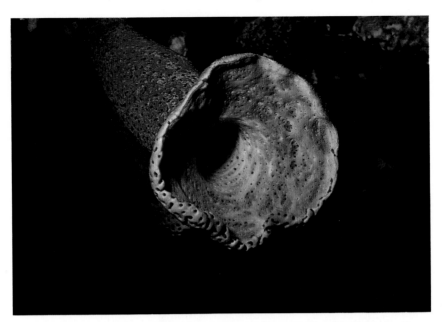

A large sponge projects outward from a vertical drop-off, showing the holes it uses for water circulation. Symbiotic zoanthid anemones (purplish-brown dots) are also visible, embedded in its outer surface. Photo: G.S. Lewbel.

Peacock flounders (Bothus lunatus) can be spotted on the sand, although they are often well camouflaged. Photo: G.S. Lewbel.

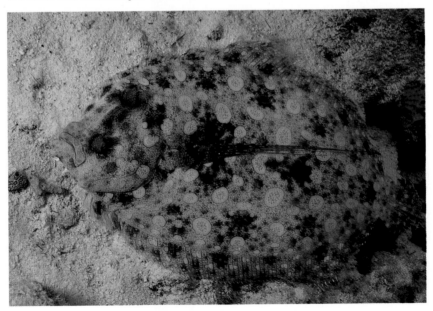

St. Elisabeth Hospital (St. Elisabeth Gasthuis), telephone 624900, has a four-person, double-lock recompression chamber. The hospital is on the Punda side of downtown Willemstad between J. H. J. Hamelbergweg, Breedestraat, and Pater Eeuwensweg. The chamber is staffed by a group of very well-qualified cardiac and pulmonary specialists, and has an ample supply of oxygen and compressed air.

Other telephone numbers that might be needed are **ambulance, 625822; emergency police assistance, 44444; and U.S. Consulate, 613066** (for help with lost passports and other paperwork problems).

Fire coral (Millepora complanata) *rims the top of a drop-off at Punti Piku.* *Photo L.R. Martin.*

Ringed anemone (Bartholomea annulata) *in a brilliant orange sponge. Photo: G. S. Lewbel.*

DAN. The Divers Alert Network (DAN) operates a 24-hour emergency number **(919) 684–8111** (collect calls accepted if necessary) to provide divers and physicians with medical advice on treating diving injuries. Many emergency room physicians are not aware of the proper treatment of diving injuries. If you find yourself or your buddy in an emergency room with a diving injury, it is highly recommended that you have the physician contact DAN. DAN will have a doctor specializing in diving medicine consult with the emergency room physician. In addition, DAN can give you up-to-date information on the location and telephone number of the nearest recompression chamber accepting sport divers. This varies from time to time so be sure to check with DAN.

DAN is a publicly supported not-for-profit membership organization. Membership is $15 per year and includes the DAN Underwater Diving Accident Manual ($4 purchased separately) describing symptoms and first aid for the major diving-related injuries, and the newsletter "Alert Diver" which discusses diving medicine and safety. DAN members are also able to buy a $25 medical insurance policy which covers hospitalization, air, ambulance and recompression chamber treatment for diving injuries. Divers should check with their insurance companies since many will not cover specialized treatment for diving accidents.

DAN's address is : Divers Alert Network, Box 3823, Duke University Medical Center, Durham, NC 27710. Their non-emergency number is (919) 684-2948.

Hazardous Marine Animals

Barracudas. Barracudas are included in this section only because of their undeserved reputation for ferocity. You'll be lucky to get one close enough for a good photograph. They're rather timid about coming closer than a few yards. At night, you can sometimes get within touching distance of a sleeping barracuda.

Bristle Worms. Bristle worms (also called fire worms) can be found on most reefs. If you touch one, it will embed tiny stinging bristles in your skin and cause a burning sensation that may be followed by the development of a red spot or welt. The sensation is similar to touching fire coral or one of those fuzzy soft-looking cactuses on land. The bristles will eventually work their way out of your skin in a couple of days. You can try to scrape them off with the edge of a sharp knife or pull them off with adhesive tape. Cortisone cream helps reduce local inflammation.

Feather duster worms (Sabellastarte magnifica) *are light sensitive, but may be photographed easily if a diver approaches without shading them. Photo: G. S. Lewbel.*

Large bristle or fire worms (Hermodice carunculata) *are abundant at Wet Suit City. This one has its white, stinging setae erect as a not-so-gentle hint to leave it alone. Photo: G. S. Lewbel.*

Eels. Moray eels are dangerous only if harassed. There are lots of morays under coral heads an in crevices, and cornered eels will bite. A bite calls for a trip to the doctor. Bites often infect.

Fire Coral. Fire coral is most common in shallow water along the terraces above dropoffs, but can grow as an encrusting form on dead gorgonians or coral at any depth. Contact with fire coral causes a burning feeling which usually goes away in a minute or two. In some individuals, contact results in red welts. Cortisone cream can reduce the inflammation. Coral cuts and scrapes also can irritate and frequently infect. Minor coral scratches can be treated successfully with antibiotic cream, but serious cuts should be handled by a doctor, especially if broken bits of coral are embedded in the wound.

Scorpion Fish. These fish are quite common in the Netherlands Antilles. They are well camouflaged, usually less than a foot (30 centimeters) long, and have poisonous spines hidden among their fins. They are often difficult to spot because they typically sit quietly on the bottom, looking more like plant-covered rocks than live fish. As with sting rays, watch where you put your hands and knees, and you're not likely to meet one the hard way. If you get stung, severe allergic reactions are quite possible, and great pain and infection are virtually certain. Add heat as for sting ray wounds, and head for the hospital and see a doctor.

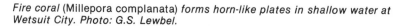

Fire coral (Millepora complanata) *forms horn-like plates in shallow water at Wetsuit City. Photo: G.S. Lewbel.*

*An agariciid plate coral
and an orange sponge
compete for space. Photo:
G.S. Lewbel.*

Sea Urchins. As in the rest of the Caribbean, the most common hazardous animal that divers will encounter in the Netherlands Antilles is the long-spined sea urchin. In fact, the species name reflects its home here: the urchin's scientific name is *Diadema antillarum*, meaning diadem or crown of the Antilles. This urchin has spines that can penetrate wetsuits including boots and gloves. Injuries are nearly always immediately painful, and sometimes infect. Urchins are found at every diving depth, although they are more common in shallow water near shore, especially under coral heads. At night the urchins come out of their hiding places and are even easier to bump into. Minor injuries can be treated by extracting the spines (it's worth a try, though they're hard to get out) and treating the wound with antibiotic cream; make sure your tetanus immunization is current. Usually, spine bits fester and pop out several weeks later. Some people feel that crushing an embedded spine (ouch!) will make it dissolve faster in the tissues. Serious punctures will require a doctor's attention.

Ringed anemone (Bartholomea annulata) *in a giant brain coral* (Colpophyllia natans). *Photo: G.S. Lewbel.*

Sea Wasps: A Hazard for Night Divers. Speaking of night diving, do avoid sea wasps! Sea wasps are small jellyfish, usually less than 6 inches (15 centimeters) long, that pack a tremendous wallop in their tentacles. Sea wasps are transparent and shaped like an elongated cube (hence the family name, *Cubomedusae*). They have four stubby tentacles. They live in very deep water during the day but swim to the surface at night to feed. They are apparently attracted to lights and gather just below the surface, where they catch other invertebrates and fish. To reduce your chances of getting stung on a night dive, wear gloves and a full wetsuit or other protection, don't snorkel or linger near the surface, and look for sea wasps before you jump into the water or make your ascent. Try cortisone cream to reduce inflammation. If the condition persists or any symptoms of allergy are present, seek medical attention immediately.

Sharks. Sharks are not common at any of the sites mentioned in this book. It would be a rare occurrence to see a shark once out of hundreds of dives, but if you do see one, it will probably be a nurse shark sleeping under a ledge. Don't worry—they eat shellfish, not divers—but don't hassle them because they wake up grumpy and have bitten a number of divers in other locations. Any shark injury calls for immediate medical attention, obviously.

Sponges. Sponges also have fine spicules, and some species have a chemical irritant that is immediately painful. You'll be pleased to know that the species name of one of the worst, *Neofibularia nolitangere*, means "do not touch." Although their brownish-red color is sometimes a clue to the bad ones, it's not completely reliable. Tiny white worms live on *Neofibularia* and can help you spot it. I have been stung by various innocuous-looking sponges. If you get spicules in your skin, you can try the same tricks I suggested for fire worms, or douse the skin with mild vinegar or mild ammonia (this sometimes works, sometimes not). The stinging sensation usually goes away within a day, and cortisone cream helps.

Sting Rays. Sting rays can be seen in sand flats. There are two Caribbean species: the southern sting ray (very large, diamond-shaped, and difficult to approach) and the yellow sting ray (small, shaped like a hubcap, and easy to approach). The southern sting ray seems more common around Curaçao. Neither will attack, but they don't like being sat on, stepped on, or prodded. They often are partially covered with sand, so look before you settle down on sandy bottoms. The long barbed stinger at the base of the tail can inflict a serious wound. Wounds are always extremely painful, often deep and infective, and can cause serious symptoms including anaphylactic shock. If you get stung put hot packs against the wound (as hot as you can safely stand). Then head for the hospital and let a doctor take care of the wound.

Appendix 1

Dive Services_____

(Courtesy Curaçao Tourist Board)
Local Numbers in Parentheses

Underwater Curaçao
Bapor Kibra
Willemstad
011-599-9-(616666) or
011-599-9-(616670)

Las Palmas Reef Divers
Las Palmas Hotel & Vacation
  Village
Piscaderabaai
Willemstad
011-599-9-(625200)

Coral Cliff Diving
Coral Cliff Hotel
Santa Martha Bay

Dive Curaçao
Princess Beach Hotel
Martin Luther King Blvd. #8
Willemstad
011-599-9-(614944)

Piscadera Watersports
Curaçao Caribbean Hotel
Piscaderabaai
Willemstad
011-599-9-(625000)

Masterdive Scubashop
Fokkerweg 13
Willemstad
011-599-9-(654312)

Masterdive Scubashop
Beaquarium
Bapor Kibra
Willemstad
011-599-9-(616666) or
011-599-9-(616670)

A small white sponge with bristling spicules is living on a larger encrusting orange sponge. Photo: G.S. Lewbel.

INDEX

*Boldface numerals indicate illustrations.